VERSUS

TESLA VS EDISON
AN ELECTRIC FEUD

KENNY ABDO

Fly!
An Imprint of Abdo Zoom
abdobooks.com

abdobooks.com

Published by Abdo Zoom, a division of ABDO, P.O. Box 398166, Minneapolis, Minnesota 55439. Copyright © 2023 by Abdo Consulting Group, Inc. International copyrights reserved in all countries. No part of this book may be reproduced in any form without written permission from the publisher. Fly!™ is a trademark and logo of Abdo Zoom.

Printed in the United States of America, North Mankato, Minnesota.
102022
012023

Photo Credits: Alamy, Getty Images, Shutterstock, Unsplash,
©Chris Light p.8/ CC BY-SA 3.0
Production Contributors: Kenny Abdo, Jennie Forsberg, Grace Hansen
Design Contributors: Candice Keimig, Neil Klinepier, Laura Graphenteen

Library of Congress Control Number: 2021950286

Publisher's Cataloging-in-Publication Data

Names: Abdo, Kenny, author.
Title: Tesla vs. Edison: an electric feud / by Kenny Abdo.
Other title: an electric feud
Description: Minneapolis, Minnesota : Abdo Zoom, 2023 | Series: Versus |
    Includes online resources and index.
Identifiers: ISBN 9781098228651 (lib. bdg.) | ISBN 9781098229498 (ebook) |
    ISBN 9781098229917 (Read-to-Me ebook)
Subjects: LCSH: Tesla, Nikola, 1856-1943--Juvenile literature. | Edison, Thomas A.
    (Thomas Alva), 1847-1931--Juvenile literature. | Electrical engineering-
    History--Juvenile literature. | Technological innovations--Juvenile literature. |
    Electrification--History--Juvenile literature.
Classification: DDC 338.7--dc23

TABLE OF CONTENTS

Tesla vs. Edison 4

The Companies 8

Fight! 14

Legacy 18

Glossary 22

Online Resources 23

Index 24

With more than 1,000 **patents** between the two men, Nikola Tesla and Thomas Edison were two of the most energetic inventors of all time!

In the late 19th century, Edison and Tesla were in a heated duel to create the best electricity system. It was known as the War of the Currents. And it was a feud that lit up America!

THE COMPANIES

Thomas Edison was born in Ohio in 1847. He tinkered and invented throughout his childhood. Before his 30th birthday, Edison set up a laboratory in Menlo Park, New Jersey.

The inventions to come out of the lab amazed the public. This earned Edison the nickname "the Wizard of Menlo Park."

Edison beside his second phonograph in 1878.

Nikola Tesla was born in Croatia in 1856. He sailed to America in 1884. Tesla began his career working with Edison. Edison had been working on a **direct current (DC)** electricity system so people could use his light bulbs in their homes.

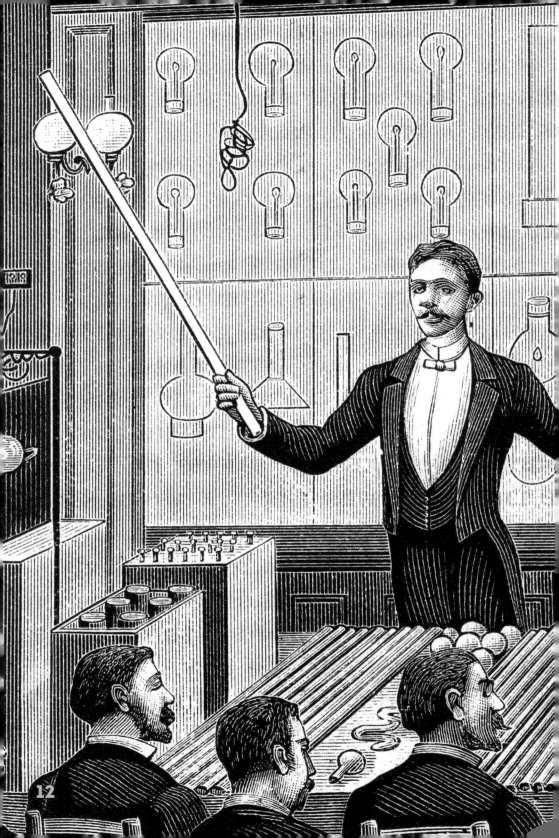

Tesla was excited to show his boss something he had been working on too. It was a motor to power an **alternating current (AC)** electric system. But Edison rejected the idea.

13

FIGHT!

Tesla then bet that he could make Edison's **DC prototype** work better. He won, but Edison refused to pay up. This pushed the two into their famous rivalry.

A.C. Transformer

Tesla quit Edison's lab. He then founded the Tesla Electric Light Company. There, he created many successful **patents**. This included the Tesla Coil, **transformers**, and **AC** motors.

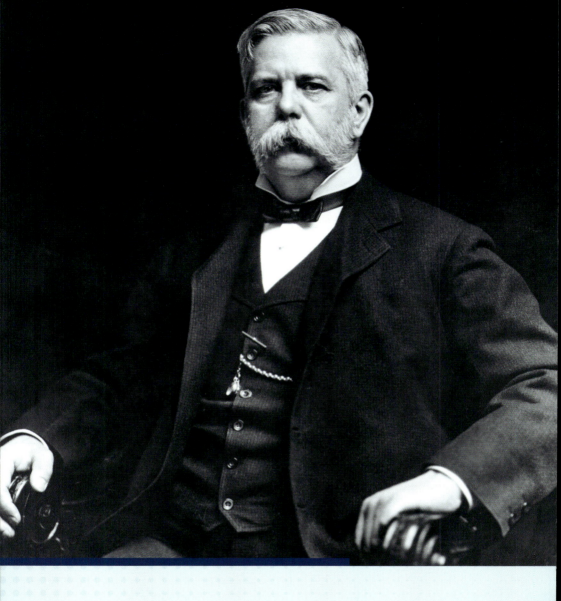

Tesla ended up selling his **patents** to George Westinghouse, who had been feuding with Edison as well. The partnership popularized **AC**, leaving Edison even more bitter.

Edison tried to discredit **AC** by spreading misinformation. He said that it was a dangerous system. In the end, AC proved to be the better and safer system. It won the War of the Currents.

LEGACY

Tesla became known for more than helping power **AC**. He was granted more than 100 U.S. **patents**. Modern inventor Elon Musk even named his electric car and **clean energy** company after Tesla.

Aside from **DC**, Edison was a **prolific** inventor. His designs included the phonograph, microphone, and motion-picture equipment!

Tesla and Edison's feud ended more than a century ago. Through their clashes, they were able to motivate each other to make the world a better place. Their inventions continue to light the world today!

GLOSSARY

alternating current (AC) – electrical charges that move in one direction and then the reverse direction.

clean energy – energy that comes from sources that do not pollute the earth.

direct current (DC) – electrical charges that flow in the same directions.

patent – a record that gives someone the right to make or sell an invention.

prolific – creating many new works or ideas.

prototype – an early model of an idea or product.

transformer – an important part of electrical systems, it is a device that transfers energy from one electrical circuit to another.

ONLINE RESOURCES

To learn more about Tesla and Edison, please visit **abdobooklinks.com** or scan this QR code. These links are routinely monitored and updated to provide the most current information available.

INDEX

alternating current (AC) 13, 15, 16, 17, 19

Croatia 11

direct current (DC) 11, 14, 20

inventions 9, 15, 19, 20

Musk, Elon 19

New Jersey 8

Ohio 8

Tesla (company) 19

Tesla Electric Light Company 15

Westinghouse, George 16